To

....

From

....

....

Published by **Lion Children's Books**
www.lionhudson.com
Part of the SPCK Group
SPCK, 36 Causton Street, London, SW1P 4ST

ISBN 978 0 7459 7942 7

First edition 2023

A catalogue record for this book is available from the British Library

Printed and bound in China, September 2022, LH54

Produced on paper from sustainable forests

Bob Hartman's ACT-ALONG BIBLE

Illustrated by
Estelle Corke

LION
CHILDREN'S

HOW TO USE THE ACT-ALONG BIBLE

Wherever I go, I meet many children (and adults) who love getting involved in the telling of stories. Active participation is at the heart of this *Act-Along Bible*! So how does it work?

My hope is to make the interaction as seamless as possible, so that the stories will flow naturally between the narrator and those taking part. Each story is a script for a narrator. The narrator encourages the audience to join in with various actions. At the beginning of each story, there is a key to describe which character the narrator will play and the role of the participant(s). It will be helpful to share this information with the child or children who are acting out the story with you. Knowing the role will help you all to think about what kind of voice to use, or even what kinds of props or costumes you may want to use – although it is just as effective to imagine and pretend without.

The bits in bold are the interactions the narrator makes with the audience, for example, actions you will want those taking part to do.

So if the line reads:

🖐 **You look puzzled…**

… then that is the cue for everyone to make a puzzled expression.

Or maybe the line is:

🖐 **Go on, swing that sword!**

That is the cue for them to swing a pretend sword. If you are doing one of these stories with your child or children for the first time, it will be helpful to run through a couple of actions or repeated phrases beforehand, so that they get the hang of it. It might even be helpful for you to lead them in their words or actions for the first story or two. Once they have caught on, you can then feel free to play your part and let them play theirs. Do pause where necessary for those taking part to enjoy doing the action or saying their words.

I hope you all enjoy the stories as you immerse yourselves in them through the things you say and do. So, "Lights! Camera! Action!"

Welcome to the *Act-Along Bible*!

Bob Hartman

CONTENTS

OLD TESTAMENT

NEW TESTAMENT

CREATION

Narrator: storyteller

Participants: Creation

In the beginning, there was God the Father, God the Son, and God the Holy Spirit.

When God created the heavens and the earth, there was only darkness.

Even darker than when you shut your eyes.

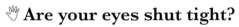 **Are your eyes shut tight?**

God's Spirit hovered above deep waters.
Then God said, "Light!"

So open your eyes.

There light was. Bright and white and blazing!

So God separated the two. He called the dark "night", and "day" is what he called the light.

And God said that it was good.

Let's say, "Good!" with him and give a thumbs up. *(repeat "Good!")*

That was the first day.

Again God spoke: "Make a space between the waters." Some waters he sent up high to make the heavens.

✋ Look up!

And some he sent down low to make the seas.

✋ Look down!

And that was the second day.

God spoke again: "Gather the waters! Make the dry land appear!"

He called the dry land "earth".

✋ Stamp your feet on the ground.

And he called the gathered waters "sea".

✋ Let's dive and splash.

"Grow!" God said next. In reply, flowers and trees, filled with fruit and seeds, burst right out of the ground.

✋ Blossom like a flower.

And God said they were good.

🖐 Let's say, "Good!" with him and give a thumbs up. *(repeat "Good!")*

That was the third day.
Then God said, "Sun."

🖐 **Put on a pair of sunglasses.**

God said, "Moon."

🖐 **Look through a telescope.**

God said, "Stars."

🖐 **Twinkle your fingers.**

There was light for the day and light for the night and signs for the seasons as well.

And God said it was good.

✋ **Let's say, "Good!" with him and give a thumbs up.** *(repeat "Good!")*

And that was the fourth day.

Then God said, "Sea creatures." And, thrashing and splashing, they multiplied, filling the waters with life.

✋ **Swim like a fish.**

Then God said, "Birds." And into the skies they came, crying and flying. Then, nesting and resting, they made little birds as well.

✋ **Fly like a bird.**

And God said that it was good.

✋ **Let's say, "Good!" with him and give a thumbs up.** *(repeat "Good!")*

That was the fifth day.

And that is when God called for the animals – wild animals, farm animals, creepy crawly animals – in all their variety and beauty and wonder.

🖐 **Which animal would you like to be? Let's hear you.**

God said they were good.

🖐 **Let's say, "Good!" with him and give a thumbs up. *(repeat "Good!")***

"And now," God said, "it is time to make people. Make them in our image. To care for the plants and the birds and the fish. To care for the animals too. And to care for each other and fill up the earth with their children."

✋ **Shake hands with one another in friendship.**

God said that it was very good. And that means you, too!

✋ **Let's say "Very good!" with him and give a thumbs up.** *(repeat "Very good!")*

That was the sixth day.

And on the seventh day? God rested. And it's important for us to rest too.

✋ **So yawn, stretch your arms, and pretend to go to sleep.**

Feels good, doesn't it?

✋ **So let's say it one last time with a thumbs up, of course: "Very good!"** *(repeat "Very good!")*

ADAM AND EVE

  Narrator and participants: angels guarding the Tree of Life

Come on!

 Wave that fiery sword.

We have a job to do here. The Tree of Life won't protect itself!

 You look puzzled.

Right, I'll go over it again. The Creator made this beautiful world.

✋ Why are you acting like a bunny?

Because you like bunnies. Yes, he made bunnies too. And then the Creator made Adam and Eve, and he gave them this amazing garden to live in.

✋ You're being a bunny again.

Yes, there are bunnies in the garden.

The Creator said Adam and Eve could eat from any tree in the garden except for the Tree of the Knowledge of Good and Evil.

✋ Wave your sword!

If Adam and Eve did that, they would die.

Then the serpent came along.

✋ You're booing and hissing.

Very appropriate. The serpent is the baddie. It told Eve that the Creator was wrong. They wouldn't die if they ate from the tree. He just wanted to stop them from knowing what he knew.

✋ You're scowling now.

Yes, the serpent told a lie.

✋ Wave that sword!

Eve believed the serpent. So she took a bite of the fruit of the Tree of the Knowledge of Good and Evil. Adam did too.

And the first thing they realized was that they were naked.

✋ **You're hiding your eyes now.**

They hid their bodies with clothes made from fig leaves. When the Creator came looking for them that evening, they hid themselves away.

✋ **You're being a bunny again.**

No, they didn't hide in a bunny burrow.

It didn't take the Creator long to figure out what happened.

✋ **You're looking worried.**

You're right! He wasn't pleased.

✋ **Wave the sword.**

He told the serpent that it would have to crawl on the ground.
He told Eve that having children would be hard.
And he told Adam that growing his own food would be hard too.
Then he sent them out of the garden home that he'd made for them.

✋ **You're looking sad.**

So you should. Adam and Eve made their lives so much harder by doing what they wanted to do instead of doing what the Creator told them.

But there is a bright side.

So you can smile a little.

The Creator told them that one day a child would be born who would bring an end to the serpent and his lies for ever.

You look confused.

No, I don't know who that child is either.

So in the meantime, we'll guard the Tree of Life, like he told us.

So wave that sword!

And yes, I see it.

Mind the bunny!

NOAH

 Narrator: Noah

 Participants: one of Noah's sons

 Grab your saw and cut that wood.

How long should it be, you ask?

 Hold out your arm. Look at it.

The distance between the tip of your middle
finger and your elbow is a cubit. And
God told me that our boat needs to
be 300 cubits long, 50 cubits wide,
and 30 cubits high. You and your
brothers will be doing a lot of sawing!

 **Now pick up your hammer and
pound in the nail.**

Pound it hard. Pound it sure.
We can't have any leaks.

The neighbours are laughing – I know.

 Put your hands over your ears if that helps.

No seas around here, they say. Why would you build a boat?
Because God told me to, I say, and they laugh even harder. They
hardly believe that God exists. And they certainly live like he doesn't.
So everything we do is a joke to them.

But this is no joke.

✋ Look up. Look down. Look all around.

People have made a mess of God's world. So he's going to start all over again. And he's going to start with us!

Right, then – time to gather the animals. Two of each. One male. One female. That's what God told me.

✋ Tell me, which animals would you like to collect?

Okay, time to lead them all in. Are you ready?

That elephant is swinging its trunk.

✋ Duck!

That camel is kicking like it's got the hump.

👋 **Jump!**

There's a spider crawling up your leg.

👋 **Brush him off. Carefully!**

And watch where you walk.

👋 **Lift your feet.**

You don't want to squash a slug
or squish a bug.

Everybody's in. And no, we don't need to
shut the door. God says that he will do it –
to make sure that we're safe and secure.

Can you hear the rain?

👋 **Make a pitter-patter sound.**

Now listen – it's raining harder.
And now it's raining harder still.
And there's thunder.

👋 **Go "boom"!**

And lightning!

👋 **Go "crash"!**

And the rivers and the seas are starting
to rise. Can you feel it? The boat has begun to rock.

👋 **Rock along with it.**

Up we go, wave by splashing wave. And now we
are floating on a sea that will cover the world!

👋 **Make a floating motion.**

Yes, I know that it feels like we have been here for ever.
   But the rain has only been falling for forty days and nights.

So let's go and feed the animals, shall we?

🖐 **Scatter the grain.**

🖐 **Hold out the hay.**

   Mind your fingers. That lion bites!
   And now we wait.

🖐 **We go to sleep and snore.**

🖐 **We wake up and stretch.**

   Again and again and again.
   Until the water subsides.

✋ **Send out a raven. Let him fly.**

Look, he's back. No land yet.

✋ **Send out a dove. Let him fly.**

Look, there's a twig in his mouth.

✋ **Pick it out and have a look.**

The water is starting to drain away.
And now, did you feel it?

✋ **A bump!**

✋ **A thump!**

✋ **A jump!**

The boat has landed!

Everybody out now.

🖐 **Smell the clean air!**

🖐 **Sway your arms in the breeze.**

🖐 **Stamp your feet on the land.**

🖐 **Wave goodbye to the animals.**

🖐 **And look up in the sky and trace the shape of that rainbow with your finger.**

What beautiful colours!

🖐 **Can you name them?**

It's a sign of God's promise that he will never flood the earth like this again.

🖐 **So let's bow our heads and thank him.**

Thank him for his brand new world!

ABRAHAM

 Narrator and participants: Abraham's servants

✋ **You're wiping the sweat from your forehead.**

Me too. It's a hot one.
But this little garden for our mistress Sarah won't plant itself.

✋ **So you keep digging.**

✋ **And now you're grumbling.**

Yes, I know Master Abraham is just sitting there in front of his tent. But this is our job, not his. And besides, it looks like he has guests. Three of them.

✋ **You're looking puzzled.**

No, I don't know who they are. But they must be very important! Look, he's bowing.

✋ **And now you're bowing too!**

Why? All right, I guess you can never be too careful.
Now Master Abraham is up on his feet. He's coming this way!

✋ **Quick, back to the digging!**

No, wait − he's going into the tent to talk to our mistress.

✋ **Put your hand to your ears to listen in.**

My hearing is rubbish. What does he want?

✋ **You say, "Cakes."** *(repeat)*

He wants her to make cakes for the guests.

And now he's running off somewhere. I say "running", but he's 100 years old!

✋ **Yes, it's more like a wobbly trot, as you're doing.**

Well, this could take a while.

✋ **Back to the digging.**

That took far less time than I thought. Master Abraham has brought them cheese, milk, and what looks like a very nice cut of beef.

✋ **You're drooling.**

Stop it. Our dinner time won't come around for ages!

✋ **And now you're sniggering.**

What's that about? The three men told Abraham what? That they would be back next year and by then Sarah would have a baby? You must be mistaken. She's ninety years old! And now somebody else is laughing. It's Sarah. Looks like we weren't the only ones listening in.

✋ Look down at the ground. Look busy!

What's that? The three men aren't impressed? They want to know why Sarah laughed? She said she didn't. They said she did.

"Nothing is too hard for God." Is that what they said?

So I guess that even a ninety-year-old lady can have a baby, if that's what God wants. And you know what that means, don't you? With a bigger family, they're going to need a bigger garden.

✋ So get digging!

JACOB AND ESAU

 Narrator: Rebecca

 Participants: Jacob

🖐 **Put your hand to your ear and listen, my boy.**

I have something to tell you. Your father, Isaac, has just sent your brother Esau off to kill something and make him a meal. When that is done, Isaac will give Esau his blessing and Esau will rule over our family when Isaac dies.

🖐 **You look sad.**

We both knew this day would come, but seeing as your father is old and blind, I have come up with a clever plan!

🖐 **Bring me two goats from our flock. Carry them. Lead them.**

Whatever way you like. But do it quickly!

Excellent! Now, as you can see, I'm cooking up these goats and making your father exactly the kind of meal he likes. Then you will pretend to be Esau, take it to him, and receive his blessing instead of your brother.

Sorry, you were mumbling. I didn't hear you.

🖐 **Say it out loud: "But Esau is a hairy man and I am a smooth man."** *(repeat)*

No worries. I have a plan for that too. I'm going to
wrap this goatskin around your neck and your hands. Stand still.

🖐 **You have a disgusted look on your face.**

🖐 **You're fidgeting.**

🖐 **And now you're scratching.**

This is going to work. Trust me.
Now, you'll also need to put on Esau's clothes.

🖐 **You look puzzled.**

So you'll smell like him, that's why!

🖐 **So put on his robe.**

That's it.

🖐 **And his favourite hat as well.**

🖐 **Now hold out your hands.
Take the platter of goat meat.**

Yes, it's heavy.

🖐 **And carry it to your father.**

🖐 **I can see that big smile on your face.**

The plan worked, did it? Show me how it went!

🖐 **You walked into the room, carrying the meal.**

🖐 **You said, "I am Esau, your firstborn son. Here is the meal you asked me to make." *(repeat)***

Then Isaac asked you how you did it so quickly. Hmmm.

🖐 **You said, "God helped me." *(repeat)***

Excellent!

Then he asked you to come near and felt your hands.

✋ **You're still scratching!**

He said what? That your hands felt like Esau's but your voice sounded like Jacob's? Rats! The old man has still got his hearing. Should have thought of that.

So he asked you if you were really Esau, did he?

✋ **And you said, "I am."** *(repeat)*

Well done.

✋ **Then you served him the food.**

✋ **You poured him some wine.**

He gave you one last sniff, just to be sure.

And he blessed you!

Result! Now you will be in charge of the family when he dies.

✋ **You're looking nervous. And now you're trembling.**

What's that? Esau's back?

No, he's not going to be happy when he finds out what we've done.

✋ **So I suggest you run!**

MOSES IN THE BULRUSHES

 Narrator: Moses' sister

 Participants: a friend who has come to see what she is doing

🖐 **Put your finger to your lips and repeat after me: "SHHH."** *(repeat)*

🖐 **Now pull the reeds apart – the ones in front of your face.**

Do you see the basket floating in the water? Don't say anything.

🖐 **Just nod your head if you do.**

My little brother is in that basket.

✋ **You look puzzled.**

✋ **Go on, say it: "Why would somebody put a baby in a basket?"** *(repeat)*

Because my mother is very clever. Hebrews like us are slaves here in Egypt, right? And Pharaoh, who rules this land, thinks there are too many of us. So he says that every baby Hebrew boy must be put to death.

✋ **I can see that sad look on your face.**

It's awful, isn't it? So my mother made a basket. She put tar on the bottom of the basket, so it would float and keep the water out. Then she put it in the river among the reeds, where no one would think of looking for a baby Hebrew boy. And she left me here to watch out for him.

Look! Someone's coming!

👋 **Duck!**

Oh, no! They're Egyptian ladies. One of them is pointing at the basket. Another one has gone to fetch it.

Now they're opening it. They found him. And he's crying!

I'm crying too.

👋 **And so are you.**

They'll kill him for sure. Listen!

✋ Put your hand to your ear.

Do you hear it? The Egyptian lady feels sorry for my brother! She wants to raise him as her own. But she needs someone to nurse him first.

✋ Jump up and down! Wave your arms!

Yes, we've got her attention!

✋ Now sit back down and wait here.

I have an idea!

Thanks for waiting. Why am I holding my brother? No, she didn't give him back. But I told her that I knew the perfect woman to nurse him. My mother, of course!

Oh, and the Egyptian lady gave him a name. It means "pulled out" because she pulled him out of the water.

✋ Maybe you'd like to say it with me: "Moses." *(repeat)*

31

EXODUS

Narrator: Hebrew parent

Participants: their child

We're free, my child! The Egyptians have finally let us go!

✋ **Go on, give a great big cheer!**

So I think it's important that we never forget how we got here.

God sent Moses to speak to Pharaoh. And when Pharaoh would not listen, God sent ten plagues. Here's how we'll remember them:

One: the River Nile turned to blood and all the fish died. It was incredibly smelly.

✋ **So hold your nose and say, "Stinky!"** *(repeat)*

Two: frogs appeared everywhere!

✋ **Give a little hop and a little "ribbit"!** *(repeat)*

Three: then God sent gnats.

✋ **Smack your arm like you are smacking those gnats.**

Four: God sent flies.

✋ **Wave your hands about like you are swatting them away.**

Five: then the animals died. Sheep and camels. Cows and donkeys.

✋ **Give a little "hee-haw", then pretend to drop down dead!**

Six: there were boils next. Horrible sores.

✋ **So frown and rub your arm like it really hurts.**

Seven: the storms of hail crushed the crops.

✋ **Duck those hail stones.**

Eight: and then the locusts came, gobbling up everything green and growing.

✋ **Make a chewing sound.**

Nine: darkness followed that.

✋ **So shut your eyes tight, then wave your hands about like you are feeling your way through a dark room.**

Ten: finally, every Egyptian firstborn child died. But our children were protected because of the lamb's blood on our door frames and lintels.

🖐 **Paint the blood up and down each side of the frame, and across the top as well.**

What's wrong?

🖐 **You're pointing ahead.**

Yes, there's a sea in front of us!

🖐 **You're pointing behind.**

Pharaoh's chariots are closing in on us.

But God is faithful. He wouldn't have brought us this far just to let us die.

Moses is raising his staff.

🖐 **You're holding your stick in the air too.**

Look, the sea is parting before us!
Hurry!

🖐 **Run! Run faster! Now slip and slide along the muddy bottom.**

We made it!

🖐 **Now, turn around.**

Do you see what I see?

We are all safely ashore, but the waves are crashing down around Pharaoh and his army!

We're free! Free at last! And everyone is cheering.

🖐 **So why don't we cheer with them?**

GIDEON

 Narrator and participants: soldiers in the army of Israel

✋ **You're standing there with your fists clenched and that brave, determined look on your face.**

I get it. You want to help Gideon beat the Midianites.
And so do I. But I have to say that it is looking harder every day.
We had 32,000 men to start with.

✋ **Then we waved goodbye to 22,000 of them because they were scared.**

So we're down to 10,000 and apparently that's still too many.

✋ **You're looking puzzled.**

I don't get it either, but now we have a test. We have to drink water from the river.

✋ **You're scooping the water up in your hands, and now you're lapping it from your hands like a dog.**

A bunch of the other men are just sticking their faces in the river, but fine, I'll do it your way.

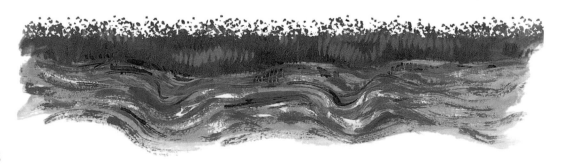

Right, now we have to walk over there with the rest of the scooping, dog-lappers. There aren't that many of us. Two, three hundred maybe?

Guess what – we're the ones who passed the test!

✋ **Okay, now you're jumping up and down.**

✋ **You're cheering.**

✋ **You're shouting, "A sword for the Lord and Gideon!"** *(repeat)*

But you do realize that out of 10,000 men, there are only 300 of us left to fight the battle, don't you?

✋ **Looking a little worried now, aren't you?**

Well, here come our weapons, and I'm even more worried.
We each have a trumpet.

✋ **Give it a blow.**

A flaming torch.

✋ **Flash it around.**

And a jar. No, I don't know what to do with that either.
Now it's night-time, and you are not going to believe our orders.

✋ **Light the torch.**

✋ **Stick it in the jar.**

✋ **Carry all that in your left hand.**

✋ **Carry the trumpet in your right hand.**

✋ **And now, very quietly, let's tiptoe down to the edge of the Midianite camp, wondering how on earth this is going to work.**

There's the signal.

✋ **So blow your trumpet.**

✋ **Smash your jar.**

✋ **Wave your torch about.**

✋ **And shout, "A sword for the Lord and Gideon!"** *(repeat)*

Now here come the Midianites out of their tents. But wait! They're sleepy. They're confused. They think they're being attacked. So they're fighting one another!

They're doing the job for us, and now all we have to do is clean up.

✋ **So grab one of their weapons. Let's give chase.**

And, yes, seeing that God has given us this victory in spite of everything…

✋ **Let's shout again, "A sword for the Lord and Gideon!"** *(repeat)*

SAMUEL

 Narrator: Eli

 Participants: Samuel

Why are you poking me, Samuel?

It's the middle of the night. I was fast asleep!
What's that, you say? My hearing is about as bad as my eyesight.

Shout out, "Did you call for me, Eli?" *(repeat)*

No, I did not.

Now run off.

That's it.

Back to bed with you.

Here you are again, boy.

You're trembling.

Yes, I know you help me
with my priestly duties and
sleep here in the tabernacle,
and to some that might seem
scary. But it's never bothered
you before.

 Say that again: "Did you call for me, Eli?" *(repeat)*

Again, I will say, "No!"

 **Now creep off back to bed. Lie down. Pull the covers over your head, if you must.**

And don't come back until morning!

You again!

 **And this time you're shaking for all you're worth.**

What's that? You heard the voice again?

There's no point sending you back until we've sorted this out.

 **So sit down. Take a deep breath.**

And let me think.

Hmmm. I might just have an answer for you.

God dwells in this place and I think it is God who has been calling your name.

So if you hear that voice again, here's what I want you to say: "Speak, Lord, your servant is listening."

 **Okay, now you say it, so you know you've got it right: "Speak, Lord, your servant is listening."** *(repeat)*

✋ **Now walk back to your bed and lie down.**

✋ **Pull those covers over your head again, if you must. Shut your eyes.**

And try to go to sleep.

Now you're back.

✋ **Jumping up and down.**

But not in a frightened way this time. You heard your name, didn't you?

✋ **I can see you nodding.**

And what did you reply?

✋ **Go on, say it: "Speak, Lord, your servant is listening."** *(repeat)*

And he spoke to you, didn't he? He told you to pass a message on to me.

✋ **You're frowning now.**

No, my sons have not been very well behaved. I didn't think the message would be good. But it's good for you, because you know what? Listening to God's message and then passing it on makes you someone very special. It makes you, young Samuel, a prophet!

DAVID AND GOLIATH

 Narrator and participants: soldiers in the army of Israel

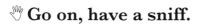 **You're trembling.**

I can see that, but you can stop trembling now. No one is asking YOU to fight the giant!

What's that, you say?

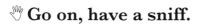 **"Who is that boy over there?"** *(repeat)*

His name is David, I think. He has brought his brothers some lovely fresh bread.

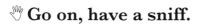 **Go on, have a sniff.**

Smells delicious!

And the cheese? Sadly, that's for the commanders. I do love a bit of cheese, though. You're right that it can be stinky.

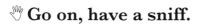 **Hold your nose.**

There goes Goliath the giant again, roaring out his challenge.

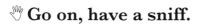 **Yes, you can put your fingers in your ears if it frightens you.**

That boy David is not frightened, though. He just volunteered to fight the giant!

He's off to tell King Saul. We've got to see this.

✋ **Come on, march along with me.**

The king has offered David his sword and armour. The boy is trying it out.

✋ **You're swinging your sword too.**

But David's not comfortable with the king's weapons. He has a different idea.

✋ **Let's follow him.**

Look! He has a sling in one hand, and he's picking stones out of that brook.

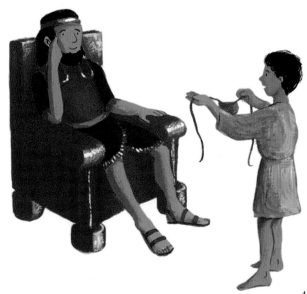

✋ **Let's count them: one, two, three, four, five!**

Now he's walking out into the middle of the battlefield.
Goliath the giant is there too, and he's angry.
He's calling David a little stick of a boy. He says he'll defeat
him and feed his body to the birds.

✋ **Now you're making an angry face too.**

And so you should. What Goliath said was not very nice.
The giant is raising his spear. Here he comes!
And now David is swinging his sling.

✋ **You're swinging as if you have a
sling too.**

Good! Out comes the stone. Aaaaaaand…

✋ **Watch as it flies through the sky…**

Bingo! It hits Goliath in the head!
He falls to the ground. David has won!

✋ **Let's jump about!**

✋ **Let's cheer and shout!**

There is a God in Israel, and
he has helped little David
defeat the giant!

ELIJAH

 Narrator and participants: people of Israel watching the contest on Mount Carmel

I see that little "Go, Elijah!" flag in your hand there.

🖐 **Yes, give it a wave.**

So that's who you're rooting for, huh?

Me, I'm not so sure.

I mean, King Ahab supports the prophets of Baal.

🖐 **You look disgusted.**

And Queen Jezebel too.

🖐 **Now you look even more disgusted.**

But most of the people of Israel support them too!

🖐 **Oh, now you just look sad.**

Well, we'll see who's right, won't we, when this contest is over.

Both sides have to make an altar. Both sides have wood. Both sides have a dead bull. And the god who sends fire to burn it all up is the true god. Sounds fair to me.

✋ **Your thumbs-up suggests you think it's fair too.**

✋ **So go ahead and wave your little flag again.**

Looks like the prophets of Baal are going first. They're calling out to Baal. They're limping around their altar.

✋ **You're rubbing your tummy.**

Yes, they've been at it all morning and now it's lunchtime. We're hungry, but still nothing has happened! And now Elijah is making fun of them.

"Perhaps your god is sleeping," he says.

✋ **You're chuckling.**

"Perhaps your god is on holiday," he says.

✋ **You're sniggering.**

"Perhaps your god is in the toilet," he says.

✋ **And you're laughing out loud.**

Well, some people might say that's not very sporting.

It has certainly revved up the prophets of Baal, though. They're dancing feverishly and cutting themselves with their swords and spears.

✋ **You're looking disgusted again.**

Who can blame you! Still no fire though, so now they're giving up.

Let's see if Elijah can do any better. He's building an altar.

✋ **You're counting the stones he's using – all the way up to twelve.**

For the twelve tribes of Israel presumably. Nice touch.

Now he's laying down the wood.

🖐 **You're waving your flag.**

He's putting the bull pieces on the wood.

🖐 **More flag-waving.**

🖐 **And now you just look shocked.**

And why wouldn't you? Because Elijah has just dumped twelve jars of water over the whole thing! For those twelve tribes again, I guess.

🖐 **That means that you're going to need to wave that flag of yours extra hard if you want that mess to catch fire.**

Now Elijah is praying.

🖐 **And you're praying too.**

(Probably better than flag-waving, to be fair.)

Would you believe it? Fire has just come down from heaven and burned up the lot – bull and wood, stones and water – everything!

No question who won that contest. Everyone is falling down on their knees and shouting, "The Lord, he is God!"

And you know what? I reckon we should join them!

🖐 **"The Lord, he is God!"** *(repeat)*

ELISHA

  Narrator and participants: two brothers

🖐 **You're wiping your eyes with the back of your hand again.**

I get it, little brother. You've been crying, and I have too.

Dad died. He owed a load of money, and now the people he owed want to sell you and me as slaves.

🖐 **Open the door, just a crack.**

I think our mother is talking to someone out there.

🖐 **Now peep through the crack.**

Who is it? Elisha? The prophet? Dad was a prophet too!

What's that? She's heading this way?

🖐 **Shut the door, quickly!**

We don't want her to think we've been spying.

🖐 **Now wave to mother. Look as innocent as you can.**

What's that? Elisha wants to help? He has an idea?

We need to go to all our neighbours' houses and borrow as many jugs and jars as we can find?

You look confused.

Me too, but if it's going to help, I'm up for it.

So open the door.

Run outside.

Slam it behind us.

And off we go.

Knock on the neighbour's door.

Ask to borrow a jar. Go on! You say it: "Can we borrow an empty jar, please?" *(repeat)*

Now grab the jar. And off we go to the next neighbour.

Knock on the door.

Ask for a jar.

Grab the jar.

Say, "Thank-you!" *(repeat)*

And off we go again!

Phew, that was a long job. But look at all the jars we got.

Your arms are full, and so are mine.

So back to the house.

Kick open the door, and put the jars on the table. Gently, so none get broken.

Right, then. What's next?

She's pouring the oil from the jar in our pantry into one of the new jars.

✋ **You're looking confused again.**

Me too! What good will it do to put the oil from one jar into another?

Hang on! The second jar is full of oil now. But the first jar is still full too! That makes no sense.

Yeah, you try it.

✋ **Pour out the oil from one jar to another. Be careful not to spill a drop.**

Look, they're both full!

Do it again.

✋ **Pour out some more.**

Same result!

✋ **Here we go, filling up every jar we borrowed with the oil from the last jar we had in the house.**

And now that the last one is full, our jar has finally run out. Amazing!

Look, Mother is headed for the door.

✋ **Open it for her.**

Watch what she does.

She's talking to Elisha again. He says that if she sells all the oil, she'll have enough money to pay off the men Dad owed and leave us plenty to live on!

I don't care if they hear us and figure out we've been listening in.

✋ **I think we should shout a big "hooray"!** *(repeat)*

DANIEL

 Narrator and participants: lions in the lions' den

I have no idea what's taking them so long! Maybe we need to growl to remind those guards that it's well past dinner time.

One, two, three…

🖐 **GROWL!**

🖐 **Look up!**

What do you see? That's right. Nothing!
I say we roar. Give it all we got!
One, two, three…

🖐 **ROAR!**

That's done the trick! They're
taking off the cover. And now
something's dropping down.

🖐 **You're drooling.**

Me too.

🖐 **So wipe your mouth.**

🖐 **Show your fangs.**

🖐 **And wave those claws about.**

Here comes dinner!

🖐 **I can hear you sighing.**

It's hardly a feast, is it? We're five hungry lions and here's one scrawny old man. Makes you weep. For us, I mean. Obviously.

Still, there's no point waiting.

One, two, three…

✋ **LEAP!**

Now what? There's this bright glowing figure standing in front of him!

✋ **Growl!**

✋ **Roar!**

✋ **Show your fangs!**

It doesn't seem frightened, does it? Now it's talking. Well, at least it speaks "lion".

It's an angel, apparently, sent here by the Maker of All Things. Our dinner's name is Daniel. He prayed to the Maker of All Things, but his enemies were jealous of him. So they got the king to pass a law that said people could only pray to him. Daniel still prayed to the Maker of All Things, and his punishment was being fed to us.

Given how skinny he is, I'd say we're the ones being punished!

🖐 **You're scratching your mane.**

Yes, it's confusing. The point is that the angel is here to keep us from eating Daniel. And given how big he is, I think we'd better do what he says.

🖐 **So zip your lip.**

🖐 **Curl up.**

🖐 **And go to sleep.**

54

Morning!

 **That's a nice big yawn.**

What did you miss? Well, the angel was pleased that we didn't eat Daniel. The king was pleased that Daniel didn't die. And I am pleased to announce that the king pulled Daniel out of our den and dropped his enemies down instead. His big, fat, juicy enemies!

 **So show your fangs.**

 **Wave those claws about.**

 **And roar!**

It's time for breakfast!

NEHEMIAH

  Narrator and participants: people rebuilding the walls of Jerusalem

Here they come again. Our enemies just won't give up.

 So wave your sword about.

No, that's not your sword – that's your trowel.

 Your sword is in your left hand. Wave it again.

And your trowel is in your right hand.

 So smooth the mortar and put a brick on top of it.

Excellent! Now they're gone.

What's that? You have a frightening trowel? A fierce trowel? A Terrible Trowel? No, I don't think that's the reason.

 You've got an annoyed look on your face.

Yes, this has been hard and dangerous work. But if we don't rebuild the walls of Jerusalem, we will have no protection at all. That's why Nehemiah came all the way from Persia. That's why he brought all that timber with him.

 Now you're looking confused.

Yes, the timber was for the gates of the city, not the walls. The gates that we have already rebuilt. And, yes, the gates have names.

You have a way of remembering the names, you say? Okay, show me.

 For the Fish Gate, you make a fishy face and a swimming motion.

✋ **For the Horse Gate, you shake your head like a horse and say, "neigh".**

✋ **For the Fountain Gate, you throw your arms in the air and make a whooshing sound.**

✋ **For the Old Gate, you pretend you're walking with a stick.**

✋ **For the Sheep Gate, you make a baaaaing sound.**

✋ **And for the Dung Gate – no, don't pretend to poo! Hold your nose and say, "Stinky!"** *(repeat)*

Better.

So we fixed the gates and now we're rebuilding the walls. Amazingly, we're almost finished, and it's only taken fifty days or so!

✋ **You're grinning from ear to ear.**

I don't blame you. We have a lot to be proud of, and thankful for too.

✋ **Why are you pointing?**

There are more enemies coming! Well, you know what to do. Wave your Terrible Trowel? I was going to say wave your sword, but all right, then.

✋ **Wave your Terrible Trowel!**

ANGELS AND SHEPHERDS

 Narrator and participants: shepherds on the hills outside Bethlehem

It's late, I know. And, yes, we're supposed to stay awake and watch the sheep.

✋ **But I can see you rubbing your eyes.**

✋ **And I can hear you yawning.**

✋ **So why don't you close your eyes, lay down your head, and go to sleep?**

I'll watch the sheep for a while along with the other shepherds.

✋ **Wake up! Wake up!**

✋ **Cover your eyes with your hands.**

That light is so bright.

It came out of nowhere! Look, it's taking the shape of something – of some kind of person. I'm terrified! I'm shaking!

✋ **You're shaking too.**

I think we should scream!

✋ **"Aaaaaaaaahhhhhhh!"** *(repeat)*

Do you hear that? The bright, light, shiny thing is talking. It's an angel!

"Don't be afraid," it says. The angel has good news for us, it seems.

That's a relief.

✋ **Yeah, wipe your forehead in relief.**

It's news that will bring joy to everyone, because today, in Bethlehem, the saviour we have all been waiting for – the Messiah – has just been born!

✋ **Shout, "Wow!"** *(repeat)*

How will we know? We must look for a baby, wrapped up in cloths and lying in a manger. Interesting!

Hang on! More bright lights.

✋ **Hide your eyes again.**

There's a whole sky full of angels. Thousands of them!

What's that they're saying?

"Glory to God in heaven above. And peace on Earth to those he loves."

I say we give them a clap.

Too late. They're gone!

Now we're off to Bethlehem to find that newborn baby.

Walking.

Jogging.

Running.

Knocking on every door.

Finally, there he is – a baby in a manger. And a mother, and a father. What's that?

You want to flap your arms like angel wings to show them what happened?

Sure, if you like.

Excellent summary. They're amazed! As well they should be. The mother is particularly impressed, nodding her head and taking it all in.

So back we go.

✋ **Walking.**

✋ **Jogging.**

✋ **Running.**

And singing like we're angels too.

✋ **"Glory to God in heaven above. And peace on Earth to those he loves."** *(repeat)*

WISE MEN

 Narrator and participants: wise men

🖐 **You're pointing up to the sky.**

Yes, I see it. A very bright and unusual star!
I'm sure it means something.

🖐 **So unroll the special scroll and let's have a look.**

🖐 **You're tapping on the scroll.**

Judea, you reckon? Way off west. And the star is a sign that a new king has been born? Well, I think we should go and have a look.

🖐 **You're holding out something in your hand.**

Gold? I see. A new king deserves presents!

🖐 **And now you're holding something else.**

Myrrh! Very expensive. An excellent choice!

🖐 **And now you're holding your nose.**

Frankincense is smelly, but I think it would make a very special present too.

Off we go!

🖐 **You're bumping up and down?**

Well, so am I, and every other wise man and his servant. What did you expect from a camel caravan?

We're here at long last, at the palace of King Herod, in Jerusalem. If anyone knows where the new king is, it will be King Herod!

✋ **Knock on the door!**

I thought that went very well. King Herod could not have been more helpful. What a nice man!

✋ **You're scowling.**

Obviously, you don't agree.

✋ **You're waving a sword around.**

Yes, I know he has a reputation for doing away with anyone who threatens his position. But you heard the man. He told us the child is in Bethlehem, and when we find him, he wants us to tell him exactly where the child is, so he can go and worship him too.

✋ **You're still scowling.**

Well, we'll deal with that when the time comes. Off to Bethlehem.

✋ **You're grumbling.**

I can hear you!

✋ **Yes, you're bumping up and down on camels again.**

But at least Bethlehem isn't far away.

✋ **You're pointing.**

Yes, there's the star. It's shining bright above this house, right here.

✋ **So knock on the door, and watch it open.**

There they are! The mother, the father, and the new king, who, to be fair, is more of a toddler than a baby. Long trip. Makes sense that he has grown a bit.

✋ **So lay the gold before him.**

✋ **And lay the myrrh too.**

✋ **And, yes, you can hold your nose while you give him the frankincense.**

✋ **Now let's all bow down and worship him.**

✋ **Let's wave goodbye.**

Off we go to rest for the night.

What are you doing? It's the middle of the night. I need my beauty sleep!

✋ **You're jumping up and down.**

✋ **You look worried.**

You've had a dream, have you?

✋ **You're waving your sword again.**

King Herod wants to kill the child, does he? So we shouldn't go back to the palace, I guess.

✋ **You're pointing at the map.**

We need to go home another way. Excellent idea!

✋ **So lay down your head and go back to sleep.**

And when morning comes, we'll avoid that evil king and do everything we can to make sure the child stays safe too!

FISHERMEN

  Narrator and participants: fishermen, who work for Simon

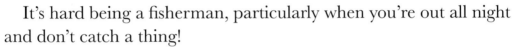

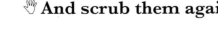 **Scrub those nets.**

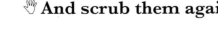 **Flip them over.**

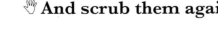 **Scrub them again.**

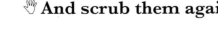 **I can hear you sighing.**

It's hard being a fisherman, particularly when you're out all night and don't catch a thing!

There are a lot of people on the shore this morning.

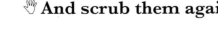 **What are you pointing at?**

I see. Jesus is here, and everyone wants to get close to him.

Hey, he's walking this way.

 Yeah, give him a little wave.

Hang on, he's talking to Simon, our boss. They are getting in our boat and pushing off from shore! Now they're stopping.

 I can see that puzzled look on your face.

But I think I know what they're up to. They're making space so everybody on the shore can see Jesus. See, he's sitting, and now he's talking. We'd better get back to work.

 So scrub those nets.

 Flip them over.

 And scrub them again.

🖐 **Phew! I can see you wiping your forehead.**

That took for ever. Long enough for Jesus to give his talk.

Simon is calling for us to join them on the boat.

Jesus wants to go fishing? In the daylight? When we caught nothing last night? Well, Simon's the boss…

🖐 **So pick up the nets.**

🖐 **Walk them to the boat.**

 **Lift them in… and drop them.**

Can't see that they'll do us much good.
Here we go.

 **Rocking back and forth.**

 **Rocking up and down.**

Out into the deepest part of the lake.

 **Pick up the nets.**

 **Drop them over the side.**

 **Hang on tight.**

Nothing happening.
But, wait a minute… something's tugging at the nets!
Hang on, don't let go.

 **Now pull! Pull with all your might.**

The nets are full of fish! Full to bursting! So full they are tearing!

 **Why are you pointing?**

Oh, I see. James and John are coming in their boat to help.

✋ **We'll pull some of the nets into our boat.**

And they'll pull some into theirs. There are so many fish that both our boats look like they might sink!

Why is Simon on his knees?

Because he doesn't think he's worthy to be around someone who has done such an amazing thing.

✋ **Let's say, "Wow!"** *(repeat)*

So what's next?

Jesus wants Simon to follow him – to leave his fishing behind. He wants to make Simon a fisher of people.

✋ **I can see that confused look on your face again.**

I don't know what that means, either.

All I can say is that if Simon is going to be a fisher of people, he is going to need some bigger nets!

THE PARALYZED MAN

  Narrator and participants: friends of the paralyzed man

 Grab a hammer.

That's right.

 Now bang it against that bit of roof until it breaks.

There you go. You've got the hang of it. You're very strong!
What was that? I couldn't hear you with all the banging.

 Say it again: "Why are we breaking up the roof?" *(repeat)*

Oh, because our friend can't walk. Jesus is in this house, you see. And we thought he might be able to heal our friend. But the house is full, and this seems to be the only way in – through the roof.

 **Keep hammering.**

That's it.

 **Just a bit more.**

 **Now pull up the broken bits and throw them over there.**

What did you say?

 **"The people don't look too happy down there."** *(repeat)*

Well, it is a good hole we've made. A man-sized hole!

 **Now grab that rope on the corner of his mat and help us lower him down.**

 **Easy. Not too fast.**

We don't want to drop him and hurt something else! There you go. Down at last.

✋ Put your hand to your ear and listen!

Jesus is talking to him. What's that?

✋ I can see by the confused look on your face that you are as puzzled as I am.

Jesus told him his sins are forgiven. Strange. I thought he would fix his legs.

The religious leaders aren't happy with what he said either.

✋ Let's listen!

They're mumbling and grumbling, saying, "Only God can forgive sins."

"What's easier?" Jesus is asking them, "to forgive a man's sins, or heal his legs?"

76

Hmmmm. I think they are both pretty difficult.

🖐 **Let's listen!**

"So to show that God has given me the power to do the one," Jesus is saying, "I'll do the other. Pick up your mat, my friend, and walk."

🖐 **Point and look!**

He's doing it! Our friend is on his feet. He's picked up his mat. He's walking! He's healed!

Everybody is cheering and praising God. I think we should cheer too. Are you ready? One. Two. Three…

🖐 **"Hooray!"**

STORM AT SEA

  Narrator and participants: disciples in a boat

Lovely day for a boat ride, isn't it?

🖐 **Take a deep breath of that fresh sea air.**

🖐 **Wiggle your fingers in the water.**

🖐 **Now put your hands behind your head, lean back, and enjoy the ride.**

Who's that over there? It's Jesus.

🖐 **You might want to put your finger to your lips and say, "SHH."**

I think he's fast asleep.

Hang on. The wind's picking up a bit. Can you feel it?
Now the boat is rocking.

 **And you're rocking too!**

You're looking a little green. How's the tummy?

 **Oh dear, there goes your lunch.**

At least you did it over the side.
The wind is getting wilder.

 **We're rocking even harder.**

And the waves are rising too. The water is washing into the boat.

 **Pick up your feet or they'll get wet.**

Too late!

 **We're rocking like crazy now. Up and down. Side to side.**

There's a very good chance we could tip over!

What's that, you say? Somebody needs to wake Jesus? Excellent idea. Go ahead. You do it.

 **You'll have to shout, "Wake up, Jesus! We're going to drown!"** *(repeat)*

Well done! He's awake.

What's he doing?

He's talking to the wind, saying, "Settle down now."
He's talking to the waves, saying, "And you need to settle down too."

 **Now we're rocking slower, and slower, and slower.**

 **Now we're not rocking at all.**

Everything is calm.

 **Put your hand to your ear and listen.**

Jesus is speaking again: "Why didn't you trust me?"

But who knew? Who knew he could do something like that?
I'm trembling at the thought of it.

 **You're trembling too.**

Who must he be if the waves and the wind obey him when
he speaks?

FEEDING 5,000

  Narrator and participants: children in the crowd

Come on! Keep up!

 Swing those arms!

 Move those feet!

 Yes, I can hear you huffing and puffing.

I'm huffing and puffing too. But Jesus is at the top of this mountain, and we want to get a good seat, right up front. Right next to him.

 Settle down!

Jesus is starting to speak now.
Let's listen to what he has to say.

✋ Was that your tummy rumbling?

✋ There it goes again.

Stop it! You're making me hungry.
Yes, we've been here ages but we're a long way from anywhere…

✋ So you can stop that moaning too.

Dinner time is not going to be any time soon.

✋ Who are you pointing at?

Isaac? Yes, who lives down the street from us. The one who can be a bit annoying at times.

✋ Yes, I can see your annoyed face.

I get it.
What's that?
He's the one whose mother packed him a lunch before we left?
Of course! He was going on and on about it.
How many fish did you say?

✋ You're holding up two fingers.

And how many loaves of bread?

✋ You're holding up five fingers now.

Well, that's more than enough for him.

✋ Run!

We'll catch him and see if he lets us have a bite or two.

✋ Swing those arms!

✋ Move those feet!

✋ Faster and faster!

Nearly there and… oh no! Looks like somebody else got to him first. Isaac is handing his lunch over to some grown-up. There goes the fish and the bread.

👋 **Yeah, you make that angry face.**

I'm not happy either. But I'm not letting some grown-up take away our – I mean, Isaac's – dinner. So let's follow him and see where he goes. We need to be careful.

👋 **So tiptoe. Tiptoe.**

👋 **Faster and faster.**

👋 **Oh, you have a shocked look on your face.**

The grown-up he handed it to is Jesus! No, I don't think Jesus would steal somebody's lunch. Look at Isaac, over there, smiling that big smile. I think he gave it away. Look, Jesus is praying now.

👋 **Yes, you can bow your head too.**

Now Jesus has a piece of fish in his hands. And he's breaking it into pieces. And he's putting the pieces in a basket.

And the basket is filling up with fish!

Now he's doing the same thing with the bread. Breaking it and filling another basket!

👋 **You've got that shocked look on your face again.**

And why not? Jesus is filling up baskets, again and again and again. With how many fish did you say?

✋ **You're holding up two fingers.**

And with how many loaves of bread?

✋ **You're holding up five fingers now.**

Look! Jesus' disciples are passing those baskets around. They're right in front of us.

✋ **Grab a piece of fish.**

✋ **Grab a piece of bread.**

It's dinner time!

✋ **Now gobble up the fish.**

✋ **And gobble up the bread.**

✋ **Now turn around and look back down the mountainside.**

There are thousands of people doing the very same thing.

So I guess Isaac wasn't so annoying after all. And Jesus was just amazing. Feeding us all with how many pieces of fish?

✋ **You're holding up two fingers.**

And how many loaves of bread?

✋ **You're holding up five fingers now.**

✋ **So pat that full tummy.**

And, yes, you know you want to do it.

✋ **Burp!**

TWO BUILDERS

 Narrator: the foolish builder

 Participants: the wise builder

Here's a story that Jesus told about two builders.
   I will be one builder, and you will be the other one.

 **You're hammering.**

And now you're sawing.

Great! But the story doesn't start like that.

It starts with digging!

That's right. The first builder – that's you – wanted to build a house. So he dug into the ground.

✋ **Get digging!**

✋ **And he dug some more.**

✋ **And he dug some more.**

✋ **And he dug some more.**

And then he hit a rock!
That rock became the foundation for his house.
He cemented bricks to that rock.

✋ **Go on! Spread the mortar, lay down the brick.**

✋ **And he laid brick upon brick upon brick.**

Then he built his house on top of that.

✋ **So now you can saw, and now you can hammer.**

When the house was finished, a storm blew up.

✋ **Go on, make a noisy, thundery storm sound.**

The nearby stream flooded and burst its banks.

✋ **Go on, make a rushing, watery sound.**

But because he'd built his foundation on the rock, his house did not shake. Not one little bit.

✋ **You look puzzled.**

What about the house I built?

Well, the second builder did not dig until he found a rock.

✋ **You look surprised.**

No, he just built his house on the sand.

And when the storm came…

✋ **You can make the storm noises again.**

And when the water rose…

✋ **You can make the flood sounds again.**

The house of the second builder fell down flat, with a great big splat!

Jesus told the story for a reason.

He said, "People who hear my words…"

✋ **Put your hand to your ear.**

"… and then do what I say are like the man who built his house on the rock.

But people who hear my words…"

✋ **Put your hand to your ear again.**

"… and then do not do what I say are like the second man.

The question is, which man do you want to be?"

THE LOST SHEEP

 **Narrator and participants:** sheep

 **I can see you yawning.**

I'm a sleepy sheep too.

 **Now you are pointing.**

What's the shepherd doing? He's counting, that's what. And he's very good at it.

But we only have two toes on each front foot, so the best we can do is count to four.

 **Go ahead, give it a go. One, two, three, four.**

What's that? He looks worried? There are supposed to be a hundred of us, and he only counted ninety-nine.

 **Now you look worried too. And you're making that sad little "baaa".** *(repeat)*

Well, I wouldn't let it keep you awake. If he's got ninety-nine here in the fold, he's hardly going to wander off into the night to search for one.

But there he goes.

 **You're baaaing again.**

You want to do what? Follow him? Out there? Where there are wolves? And bears? And thorn bushes? And every other kind of sheep-shredding thing?

All right. But we need to be quiet.

 **Creep out of the fold.**

 **Run to keep up.**

 **Duck under the branch.**

 **Jump over the log.**

 **Splash through the stream.**

Do you wish you had stayed at home yet?

 **Climb up the hill.**

 **Roll down the other side.**

 **Stop. And catch your breath.**

I think he's found something.

✋ **Creep up slowly. More slowly still, and peep down over the edge of the cliff.**

The sheep is there! It's Nigel!

✋ **Yes, you can give a happy little "baa".**

✋ **But not too loud.**

He's trapped in a thorn bush – what did I tell you? But the shepherd has set him free. He's put him on his shoulders, and they're coming this way.

✋ **Quick, hide behind that boulder!**

Now we retrace our steps.

✋ **Take a big breath.**

✋ **Climb up the hill.**

✋ **Roll down the other side.**

✋ **Splash through the stream.**

✋ **Jump over the log.**

✋ **Duck under the branch.**

✋ **Run to keep up.**

🖐 **Creep back into the fold.**

🖐 **And wave hello to Nigel.**

What's the shepherd doing? Sounds like he's throwing a party.

🖐 **Yeah, you can give the biggest, happiest "BAAA" you can manage.**

Me? I'm ready for that sheepy sleep!

JESUS AND THE CHILDREN

  Narrator and participants: children waiting to see Jesus

You're yawning again!

And, yes, I'm bored too. We've been standing here for ages. Don't get me wrong – I think Jesus is amazing. But I had no idea that it would take this long to get him to bless us.

You're scratching your head.

What does "bless" mean? I guess it means he prays for us and asks God to watch over us and help us. That kind of thing.

Why are you jumping up and down?

No, I don't think it will make you tall enough to see what's going on at the front of the queue. No, you're not climbing on my shoulders!

Maybe we should do something to pass the time. We can play catch.

Pick up that rock and throw it to me.

Not at my head! Maybe we should try playing something safer.

Draw a picture of something in the dirt with your foot.

Nice!

What's my picture? No, it's not the high priest! It's a cat!

Laugh all you want!

Drawing is not my talent.

Ooh, now we're moving. At last!

I think you need to walk a little faster.

And faster still. Now stop!

Why? Because Jesus' disciples told us to. They're not going to let us see Jesus. They say he's too busy, and that he doesn't have time to spend with kids like us!

Yeah, I can see your angry face.

I'm angry too, and we're not the only ones. Here comes Jesus, and it looks like he's angry as well!

🖐 **Put your hand to your ear and listen.**

He's telling off his disciples. He's telling them that they shouldn't keep us away.

He's telling them that he wants everyone who follows him to be like us! No, I don't think he means that they should throw rocks at each other's heads! He wants to get to know us!

Here we go.

🖐 **We're walking right up to the front of the queue.**

🖐 **Yeah, you can shout "hooray" if you like.**

Because it's time to get blessed!

ZACCHAEUS

 Narrator and participants: people from Jericho, waiting to see Jesus

 You're jumping up and down!

Yes, I know. It's hard to see. But everyone in Jericho is out here on the street. Right. Let's try again to get to the front.

 Tiptoe to your left.

 Tiptoe forward.

 Get down on all fours and crawl between that tall man's legs.

 Stand up again.

 Turn your body to the right and SQUUUUUEEEEEZE between those ladies.

 Say, "Sorry. Pardon me." *(repeat)*

And look, we've done it! We'll have no trouble seeing Jesus when he arrives!

 You're pointing.

Yes, there he is.

👋 **Yes, we can give him a little wave, if you like.**

What's that? You want to invite him to our house to have something to eat? I think that's pretty much what everyone else is doing. And hey, what an honour it would be if he said yes.

👋 **Go on, then, shout it out: "Can you come to our house to eat, Jesus? We're having boiled goat!"** *(repeat)*

Not sure you should have added that last bit. What if he doesn't like goat?

He's moving on, anyway. Now he's looking up into that tree.

👋 **Now you're pointing again.**

Yes, there's something in the tree. No, not a very large chicken. A very small man. It's Zacchaeus, the tax collector.

✋ **You've got an angry look on your face.**

Yes, he's a cheat.

✋ **You're waving your fist in the air.**

Because he collects taxes for the Romans, who have taken over our country.

✋ **Now you're stamping your feet.**

Because Jesus has just asked if he can eat at Zacchaeus' house. That can't be right. You're not the only one who's angry. The whole crowd is complaining. Who can blame them?

But off Jesus is going into Zacchaeus' very nice house.

✋ **You're crossing your arms and making that angry face again.**

Yes, we can wait. I want to see what happens too. Maybe Jesus is just telling him off.

At long last, the door is opening, and here Zacchaeus comes.

✋ **You look shocked.**

Zacchaeus is sorry for what he's done.

✋ **You look amazed.**

He says he'll pay back anyone he's cheated four times more than what he took!

✋ **You're cheering.**

He says he'll give half his money to the poor! Now everyone is cheering. And Jesus has this great big smile on his face. I guess he knew where he really needed to eat his dinner after all.

✋ **Now you're rubbing your tummy.**

Yes, it's probably time to go home and chow down on that boiled goat!

PALM SUNDAY

  Narrator and participants: the donkeys that Jesus borrows for his ride into Jerusalem

Lovely morning, Darling, don't you think?

I hear you making that happy little hee-haw sound.

We're chewing our straw.

Shaking our heads.

And flicking the odd fly away with our tails.

It's a downright delightful donkey day!
Who are these two strangers? I hope they don't spoil things.
Hang on! They're untying us!

Stamp your feet and kick your legs.

Nobody's stealing me and my colt! Wait a minute. Our master is smiling. He's giving them the thumbs up. I guess this is all right, then. Off we go.

Clip-clopping.

Shaking our heads.

Flicking away the odd fly with our tails.

Now what? There are a bunch of men around us. They're taking off their cloaks. For makeshift saddles, I'm guessing. Looks like I'll be taking one of them for a ride. But hang on, they're putting the cloaks on YOUR back!

✋ **I see that worried look on your face.**

And I get it. This is the first time anyone has ever ridden you.

✋ **You're shaking your shoulders.**

✋ **And fidgeting about.**

✋ **But you need to calm down.**

That's the best way. Besides, the man who is walking up to you seems very nice.

He's patting you on the head and telling you that everything will be fine.

✋ **Now you're doing that happy little hee-haw sound again.**

Up he hops.

✋ **You're shifting your shoulders.**

That's right, get comfortable. And off we go! Down the hill.

✋ **Clip-clopping.**

✋ **Shaking our heads.**

✋ **Flicking away the odd fly with our tails.**

Now this is strange. More people are taking off their cloaks. They're laying them in front of our feet! Ooh, feels nice. Better than the dusty road.

✋ **But pick up your hooves – we don't want to trip.**

Look! Now they're cutting palm branches from the trees and laying those in front of us as well!

✋ **Pick up your hooves again.**

They feel kind of scratchy.

And now everyone is shouting, "Hosanna to the king of Israel! Blessed is the one who comes in God's name! Hosanna in the highest!"

✋ **You look puzzled.**

Well, it's not you they're shouting about. Nor me, either.

I'm guessing it's the man on your back. And if that's the case, then he's the most unusual king I ever heard of. Riding on a donkey! Who would have guessed?

Into the city we go, at the head of the king's parade.

 **Clip-clopping.**

 **Shaking our heads.**

 **Flicking away the odd fly with our tails.**

On this downright delightful donkey day!

THE WIDOW'S OFFERING

 **Narrator and participants:** Jesus' disciples

Are you any good at counting?

✋ **I see you're nodding.**

Excellent! Well, Jesus has a counting question for us.

Do you see those people putting their offerings in the box on the Temple wall?

✋ **You're strutting about, like a proud peacock.**

Yes, some of them do look very rich. When they put their money in the box, it makes quite a clatter, so everyone around knows exactly how rich they are. And roughly how much they have given.

✋ **You look disgusted.**

So you should.

✋ **Now you're putting your finger to you lips and going, "SHHH!"**

You're right. Jesus told us that when we give, we should do it quietly and not make a big fuss so that other people see how generous we are.

✋ **You're pointing up to heaven now.**

Yes, what we give is supposed to stay between us and God.

Well, whatever the case, now Jesus wants us to say which of the people are giving the most.

 **So put your hand to your ear and listen closely.**

Here comes the first one.

 **Yes, count the coins as they drop down, if you can: one, two, three, four, five.**

So that man gave five coins.

 **Right, then – put your hand to your ear and listen to the next one.**

✋ Yes, count them out as they fall: one, two, three, four, five, six, seven, eight, nine, ten.

Well, that man gave more. Ten coins in all.

And the last person in the queue is that little old woman.

✋ You're pointing at her.

You know her, do you? She's a widow. I see. Not much money, then. And not much is likely to go into the box. Still, we need to count.

✋ So put your hand to your ear and listen.

✋ One, two.

That was easy. Just two coins. I think we have our answer.

✋ Go on, tell Jesus, "The second man gave ten coins, so he gave the most." (repeat)

✋ You look surprised.

Jesus doesn't agree. He says the widow gave the most because she gave everything she had!

✋ Now you're laughing.

Yes, I can see the funny side. Jesus has his own way of adding things up.

I guess we weren't that good at counting after all!

108

CRUCIFIXION

 Narrator: Mary Magdalene

 Participants: the other Mary

You're crying, Mary.

And I'm crying too. But we followed Jesus, way back in Galilee. And we took care of him and supported him, didn't we?

You're nodding.

You know that journey has brought us to Jerusalem and to this terrible place. I'm not giving up on him now.

You're pointing.

Yes, I see it. They have nailed him to the cross and stood it up between two others.

You're hiding your eyes.

No, I can hardly bear to watch either. It must hurt so much.

Now you're shaking your head.

111

The Roman soldiers have divided his clothes and are gambling for them, while he hangs there and dies. Disgusting behaviour!

 **You're holding your hand to your ear.**

Yes, I hear it. Some of our own people are saying some very disgusting things too. They're mocking Jesus, telling him to save himself and come down from the cross.

The religious leaders are joining in, shouting, "He saved others, why can't he save himself?" and "Come down and prove that you are the king of Israel!"

 **I hear you sighing.**

They don't understand, do they? He came to be a different kind of king than the one they all expected.

 **And – oh! – you just gasped.**

Me too! The world has suddenly been plunged into darkness. Perhaps it's a mercy that we can hardly see a thing.

Three hours have passed, and finally we can see clearly again.

 **You're looking down at the ground.**

I get it. Jesus looks so much worse. He's crying out. Someone thinks he's calling for the prophet Elijah. They've brought him some wine on a long reed. He's drinking it. Oh, and now he's crying out again. It's so awful!

✋ **Cover your ears.**

He's not moving. He's not breathing. I think it's over.

✋ **Your hands cover your face.**

✋ **We're both crying.**

✋ **And now you're pointing.**

To that soldier over there. Why him?

I see. He's looking up at Jesus, but there is no hate in his face. Listen to what he says: "This man was truly the Son of God."

He gets it!

✋ **You've got a confused look on your face now.**

"What will happen to Jesus' body?"

Well, we're in no position to claim it. Perhaps we should wait and see.

✋ You're yawning.

Yes, it's evening now, and I'm exhausted.

✋ Why have you got that smile on your face?

I see! It's Joseph, from Arimathea. Yes, he's a member of the ruling council, but he has always been sympathetic to Jesus.

He's taking down the body! He's wrapping it in a cloth! He must be taking charge of the burial! Let's follow him and see where the tomb lies.

✋ Run! Run faster!

We have to keep up, but it might also be sensible to keep out of sight.

There it is – the tomb!

✋ You're whispering now.

Yes, I think you're right. When the Sabbath has passed, we'll come back to this place and dress the body with just the right spices. It's the least we can do for our friend. And we'll have the chance to see him one last time.

RESURRECTION

 Narrator: Mary

 Participants: another Mary, who goes to Jesus' tomb

✋ **You're yawning.**

Yes, I know it's early. But look, the sun is peeping its head above the hills. At least we can see where we're going.

✋ **And yet, you tripped anyway!**

✋ **Hold on to those spices.**

✋ **Hold on tight.**

We don't want to drop them.

✋ **I can see you wiping that tear from your eye.**

Yeah, I'm sad too. We all are. Jesus was our friend and now he's gone. It's the least we can do to put these spices on his body.

We're nearly there – though how we're going to roll the stone away from the tomb, I do not know.

✋ **You're flexing your arm.**

I get it, but I don't think even you will be strong enough to move it.

Hang on. That's the tomb over there. Someone has already rolled the stone away!

✋ **I can see that puzzled look on your face.**

I'm puzzled too. Who moved it? And why? Looks like the rest of the women are going into the tomb. Oh my! I guess we should follow them.

 **Duck!**

 **Yeah, I can see that shocked look on your face.**

Jesus' body isn't here!
But somebody else is!

 **Look to your right!**

Two people all dazzling and bright!
They must be angels. They must have been sent by God.

 **So bow down!**

They're speaking: "Why are you looking among the dead for someone who is alive?"

What a strange question!

 **You're shrugging your shoulders.**

No, I don't know either.

What's that they're saying now? Jesus isn't here? Because he's risen? And he told us it would happen way back when we were in Galilee?

 **You're shaking your head.**

You can hardly believe it, and neither can I. But the angels have told us. The tomb is empty. It's amazing!

Now it looks like everyone is leaving. We have to go back to the others. We have to tell them what we saw.

 **So we walk.**

 **And we walk faster.**

 **And now we're running.**

Who can blame us? We have the most incredible news to share.

 **Yes, you can shout, "Hooray!"** *(repeat)*

PENTECOST

  Narrator and participants: followers of Jesus, praying and waiting for the gift he promised to send

🖐 **You're praying again.**

Good! It's what Jesus told us to do. Pray, and wait for the special gift he promised to send us. How many days has it been since he returned to heaven now?

🖐 **You're counting to ten.**

Feels about right.

Hang on.

🖐 **Are you making that wind-rushing sound?**

No? Well, it's coming from somewhere.

✋ **You're pointing at my head.**

And if my head looks like yours, there are flames like fire floating above it.

Look at your face!

✋ **You're beaming, like every bit of you is filled with the joy and the goodness of God.**

This must be it! The gift Jesus promised. His Holy Spirit.

✋ **Now you're talking in a foreign language.**

And yet I understand what you're saying.

✋ **You look puzzled.**

I'm assuming you can understand me too.

✋ **You're waving to me to follow you.**

Oh, I see. Everyone else in the room is going outside. So I guess we should go too.

🖐 **You look amazed.**

A huge crowd has gathered around us. People from all over the world have come to Jerusalem for the feast of Pentecost. What's that they're saying? They can all understand us talking about God's mighty works – each in their own language. Incredible!

🖐 **But you look really annoyed.**

I see – that man over there just told everyone that we were acting like this because we were drunk. Not true. Now I'm annoyed too.

🖐 **You're pointing.**

Peter has just stood up. He'll put that man right, and that's just what he's doing. He says we're not drunk.

🖐 **You're nodding your head in agreement.**

He says that God promised this would happen; that one day everyone – men and women, young and old, slaves and free – would receive God's Spirit.

🖐 **Now you're smiling.**

And he says that this is the gift of Jesus, who was raised from the dead, ascended to heaven, and now rules with God in heaven.

🖐 **You're pointing at your eyes.**

Yes, we saw him alive again. And yes, we saw him disappear into heaven! He says that this was the very same Jesus our people put to death on a cross.

🖐 **You're wiping a tear from your eye.**

You're not the only one. The crowd has gone quiet. Some people are weeping.

Someone is asking Peter what they should do.

Peter answers, "Say you're sorry for what you have done. Be baptized in the name of Jesus, the Messiah. Be forgiven by God, and you, too, will receive his Holy Spirit."

🖐 **You're pointing again.**

I see. Thousands of people are doing what Peter said!

🖐 **Now you're beaming again.**

And why not? They will experience the joy we have. And be filled with God's Holy Spirit too!

Enjoyed this?

Why not read some of Bob Hartman's other amazing books...

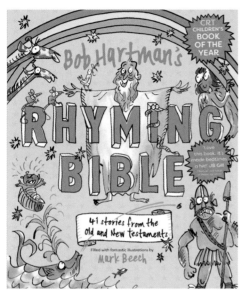

Bob Hartman's Rhyming Bible
9780281077946

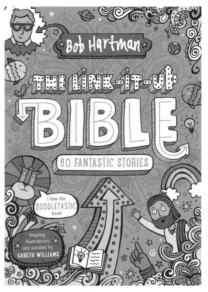

The Link-it-up Bible
9780281083022

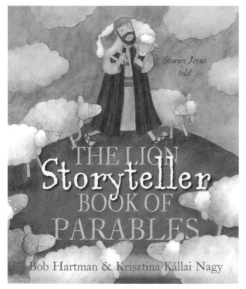

The Lion Storyteller Book of Parables
9780745964461

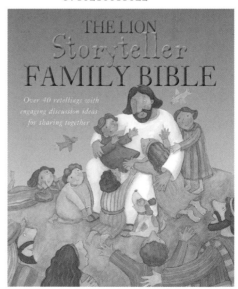

The Lion Storyteller Family Bible
9780745978420